*Penny Andrews*
*Isa. 26:3*

# This is My Story,

# This is My Song...

An Autobiography of:

Mrs. Penny Andrews

Praising my Savior all the day long...

I dedicate this book to my son, Mark.
You have filled my life with joy!

And, to the memory of my late husband,
Floyd Andrews, the love of my life.

### Foreword:

By Dave Compton and Dr. Jack Lemons

For nearly forty years, I have known Penny Andrews. I have known her as an able vocalist in Gospel music, during her years with the famed Gethsemane Quartet, and in the last serval years, since the death of her late husband, Floyd, I have observed her ministry of singing in a solo capacity. I have also known her by her artistic ability in painting beautiful pictures. I should mention, too, that I know Penny as one of the finest cooks ever! Many times, have I sat at her table. She is also a very gifted speaker, a student of God's word, and faithful to prayer.

She gets high marks as a devoted wife, mother, and grandmother. From a personal perspective, she has been my kind and dear friend for so many years. That has been a joyous gift to me.

Now, I can say that I know Penny as an author! The book that you're holding now, is her life. On occasion, I have heard much of her story through friendly conversation, and have often thought that her experiences, and her close walk with the Lord, belong in the pages of a fine book. That has now become a reality. Once you start this journey with Penny, in reading her book, it will be hard to put it down. You will walk life's road with her as she recalls her early childhood days and the present times. Not only will you really get to know Penny in a more personal way, but you will also benefit spiritually. I believe, as you read her life's story, with all the elements of her blessings, laughter, the struggles and the challenges that has strengthened her faith, you, no doubt, will find resolve in knowing that you, too, can trust Christ with your life, have confidence of His grace, His presence, and His love.

I am so proud that Penny has taken this step of documenting one beautiful life of walking with the Lord, and being a faithful witness of His gospel! Friend, be blessed as you read the life and times of one incredible woman of God, my friend, Penny Andrews.

Dave Compton
Program Manager/Morning Personality
WPET Radio
Greensboro, NC

Penny Andrews is one of the most talented people I have met in my fifty years of serving Christ. Her wit and wisdom, her compassion and courage, her faith and faithfulness, and her love for the Lord, continue to leave an indelible mark upon the hearts of the many she ministers to. Now, sit back and enjoy as Mrs. Penny shares her story and her song with you.

Dr. Jack Lemons
Former Pastor
McLeansville Baptist Church
McLeansville, NC

## Preface:

I heard a message some time ago. I don't remember where I was or who brought it. The title of the message was, "What are you doing with your DASH?" The dash represents all that transpires between the date of your birth, and the date of your death.

I've thought a lot about that question. I ask myself, "Has my life meant anything? Has it been meaningful at all? Most importantly, has it been pleasing to my Heavenly Father?"

Considering what my life has been so far, I am attempting to put some of it into words, on paper, for my children and grandchildren.

Having said this, how do I begin to fit eighty plus years of living into the pages of a book approximately 8 x 10 inches or less? Well, I am going to attempt to do just that. I know I cannot possibly begin to recall everything that I have experienced, but I will try to write about what I feel is important, and that will be of the most value.

I pray, as you read this, you will get something from it that will encourage you as you live the DASH between your two very important dates.

Ms. Penny

# Chapter One
*My Family*

I was introduced to this world on November 27, 1931, just at the end of the depression. I was born at home, about thirty minutes before the doctor arrived. This was the only time I've ever been early for anything!

**Me, when I was 3 years old**

I grew up in a cotton mill village. The name of the town was 'Revolution', named for the mill that it surrounded. There were four different mills around us, all owned by the Cone family. At that time, they were owned by Mr. Ceasar Cone. (Mr. Cone is now buried at Buffalo Presbyterian Church in Greensboro, North Carolina.) He was kind and generous to his employees. He gave every family a turkey for Thanksgiving and a ham for Christmas. All of us kids received a very nice Christmas gift from him, and a big bag with nuts, fruit, and candy at school. What a treat! You see, we only got oranges, apples, and candy once a year, and that was at Christmas. We always looked forward to the walnuts, pecans, and almonds.

I was the third child, but the first girl. I guess that's why I am so mixed up! Ha Ha! My sister, Linda, was not born until I was almost ten years old. I had two brothers older than me, Bernon, being the oldest, and Bascom was next to me. Bernon passed away at the age of fifty-six from Cancer. Bascom was three and a half years older than me and also is with the Lord.

Before I was born, my parents took in two other children, when their parents died due to a flu epidemic in the late twenties. They were my dad's sister's children. Zeno Moore was already a teenager, so he didn't stay with them very long. His sister, Rena, was only seven years old. I barely remember her being there. Sometimes I wonder if I have actual memories of her, or if I am only recalling what others have told me.

We were very poor, but we didn't know it. You see, it was right after the Great Depression, and everyone we knew was, pretty much, the same as we were. Despite what little we had, I didn't feel poor. I still marvel at how my parents were able to provide for us as well as they did. I don't remember ever going hungry. Actually, we always had ample food on our table, and always homemade desserts, with biscuits and fried meat skins in the warming closet of the stove.

My dad had a big garden, so we had fresh vegetables in the summer time. My mom canned everything she could, because, of course, we didn't have freezers. In fact, we had none of the luxuries we so often take for granted today.

I would watch my Mother early each morning pack several bag lunches and set them on our buffet, because she knew there would be people coming to our back door asking if there was any work they could do to earn a meal. They sure came to the right house when they came to ours. Those were the days you could help a stranger without fear for your life or your possessions. My, how things have changed, and not for the better!

I am amazed when I look back on my life and see how God has worked; how He has ordered events in my life to bring me where I am today.

My mom said I came into this world singing. Well, not actually singing. However, she said she would sing to me when I was a baby and I would hum in tune with her. She said people would come all over the mill hill to see this strange baby. I'm still strange! As I got older, I would sing to everything, I would pick up any bug or caterpillar and sing to it, calling them my beebee's. Mama was afraid I would pick up a spider, but the good Lord protected me.

My dad was very strict on me, much more than my brothers and even my sister, but she came along much later. I didn't understand it then, but I think I do now.

I had to sing every day of my life. My dad saw to that. Each day when I came home from school, I would have to sing and play the piano for him before I could do anything else. He would permit me to go to the movies once a week if I learned to play at least three new songs. He would even sit in the room while I took music lessons to make sure he approved of everything my teacher taught me.

On Tuesdays and Thursdays, a group of about sixteen young people, came to our house. My dad taught music by shape notes and we would sing for about two hours. Wednesdays, of course, we went to church. On Fridays, we would go somewhere to sing, then on Saturdays, I took piano lessons.

Sunday morning, I got up very early and got dressed for church because a couple of preachers and their wives would pick me up and take me to W.B.I.G. radio station to do a broadcast. I was only twelve or thirteen years old. I would play the piano for them. Then, they would bring me home and I'd walk with my family to church.

Our family would have devotions at night around the Bible. My mom would read a Bible story, then dad would read from the scriptures. Then, he would kneel down on the old linoleum-covered floor to pray. I remember kneeling beside him, watching him, as the tears flowed from his eyes, ran down his nose, and made a puddle on the floor. I can remember it all, but through the eyes of a child, not quite understanding its meaning. I have no idea how old I was at this time, but this is one of my earliest memories. What a wonderful one!

There are many other memories that fill the windows of my mind when thinking of our family. One memory is when I would get to go to the store with my father. He was not very big in stature, perhaps all of five feet and four inches. But, I was very small, too. I was small enough to stand on the top of his foot, wrapping my arms around one leg. In this position, I would "ride" all the way to, and from, the store. What a great ride!

Back then, my world was so small, we walked everywhere we went. Except, of course, on rare occasions when we would get a ride from a friend. My dad never owned a car. Thinking back on that now makes me smile, because I am so dependent on mine.

## *My House*

A car wasn't the only thing my family didn't own. There was no air conditioning, except for the air that blew through the screen windows. We had only one sink and it was in the kitchen. It only poured out cold water, because the hot water had to be boiled on the old wood stove.

Times were so different when I was a child. Life was much simpler. We lived in a four-room house with no insulation and no underpinning. In some places, you could see through the floor onto the ground below. We had heat in the kitchen and in the living room (I use that term lightly), but none in the rest of the house. When I got ready for bed, I would sit by the old wood stove in the kitchen with my feet on the enamel skirt around the bottom of it, until my feet were almost cooked. Then I would run like blue blazes to my bed across the hall, where I would have so many covers over me that I could hardly turn over all night.

A picture of our house drawn by me

The toilet in the old house was on the back, screened-in porch. And, of course, there was no heat there either. I didn't know what it was to have a bathtub until I was nineteen years old. Until then, I had bathed in a number three washtub, once a week, on Saturday. That was a hoot! The rest of the week, I pan bathed at the one sink in our kitchen. There was no hot water just by turning the spigot. The water had to be heated.

We didn't have T.V., of course, but we did have a radio. Even so, radios had not been around very long. Airplanes were also very new. I used to read in comic books about things like rocket ships, watches you could talk to, robots, and all kinds of other gadgets that, now, are a common, everyday occurrence. A lot of this futuristic stuff, I used to read about in Flash Gordon comics. Now, I use these things daily.

## *My Town*

Things were so much safer when I was a girl. We kids could play outside at night or walk several blocks to the movie theatre and never give a thought about someone attacking us. We left our doors unlocked all during the day. I think my dad locked our doors at night, but he was especially careful. I do remember one night when he let a stranger spend the night with us. He stayed in Bascom and Bernon's room. Since we only had two bedrooms, my brothers had to stay in the room with me, Momma and Daddy. We all slept on two beds, and they weren't king sized, either!

When I was eleven years old, President Roosevelt declared war on the Japanese. Then, finally, on Germany and Italy. I will never forget that day. I was across the street at a neighbor's house, playing with their kids. After that broadcast, there was no more playing. I remember all the young men who were drafted or enlisted in the service. One of them was killed, shot down. He was a pilot. Another was captured by the Japanese and tortured. I don't think he ever got over the trauma of it all. Others were wounded.

There was an army base right here in Greensboro. It was called the 'Overseas Replacement Depot' or 'ORD'. I can still hear them playing "Taps" and "Reveille". Everywhere you looked, there were soldiers.

Even the kids had a part in the war. One thing we did for the war effort was to gather as much tin foil as we could find and roll it into a ball. You see, back then, all chewing gum wrappers and cigarette packs were made of real tin foil. The government would pay us for the foil and use it to make bullets.

A lot of things were rationed during the war, such as sugar and gasoline. Also, before the war, women's hose was made of silk. Because we could no longer obtain the silk, that created a need for a substitute called 'Nylon'.

Another thing was rubber. Because of the shortage of rubber, which was being used in the war, we were given another substitute called synthetic rubber. This is still being used today. It was during this time that many new things became common place.

## *My Church*

I have another childhood memory of our church bell. Back then, most churches would have a bell in the bell tower and would ring them every Sunday morning, calling the people to worship. My dad was a deacon and a Sunday school teacher. Every now and then, it would be his responsibility to ring the bell. Since there were two ropes attached to the bell. he would let me hang on one side while he pulled down the other. This raised me up off the floor and into the air. Then, as he let his side of the rope go slack, I would come sailing back down. This was quite an adventure for me!

At this time, our church was called Revolution Baptist Church. It was a large, white-framed building on Cornwallis Drive. Now, the new church is a big, brick church across the street from the old one, and has a new name, Northside Baptist Church.

# Chapter Two
*My Love*

I never thought that I would meet anyone who loved music as much as my daddy did. He had three loves in his life: his Lord, his family, and music. He walked around with either a Bible or a song book in his hands nearly all the time.

I remember when I was eight or nine years old, lying at the foot of my bed, in front of a big screened window, saying my prayers and asking the Lord to send me someone when I was old enough to marry. I prayed he would love to sing so that I could sing for the Lord the rest of my life. I even asked God to give him black, curly hair and blue eyes. I later told Floyd that he didn't have a chance because God and I had him cornered.

It's amazing how I remember every single time that I saw Floyd, even when we were children. My cousin, Rena, who my parents raised since she was a young girl, courted Floyd's older brother, Lonnie, when Floyd and I were just babies. I grew to love Lonnie fiercely. Everywhere they went, they had to take me, if I was awake.

Occasionally, they would go down to Chatham County where Lonnie's parents lived. Of course, this is where Floyd lived also. I would tell them to tell the little boy down there that I said 'hello'. I would even send him my little Sunday school papers.

Once, they brought him to my house. We were about eight years old and I remember sitting on our front steps and talking. The next time I saw him, we were eleven years old, when his family moved from Chatham to Greensboro. I was spending time at Lonnie and Rena's house, and Floyd rode his horse over there and asked us to go back home with him. I remember that he put Bronna Mae, Rena and Lonnie's daughter, on the horse with him. She was only four or five years old. Rena and I followed them on foot. I recall drinking buttermilk at his house. Oh, the things we remember!

The next time I saw him, was my first year at Rankin High School. I was in the ninth grade and it was very early in the school year. I saw three guys racing down the hallway and recognized one of them as Floyd. I don't think he even saw me.

About a year later, Red Snyder was working with Floyd at White Oak Mill, and they had become very good friends. It was, at this time, that we were having big singings at Gethsemane Baptist Church. I was the pianist and my dad was the music director. Red Snyder sang in the choir. He knew how much Floyd loved gospel music, so Red invited him to come with him on a Sunday night to one of our big singings.

The night Floyd came, my brother, Bascom, and I sang a duet. When he saw me, he didn't recognize me, but he told Red that 'if that girl wasn't married, I'd marry her'. Red informed him that I wasn't married, and the man I was singing with was my brother. He set out to get me from that very moment. He said he loved me from the first moment he saw me. I was seventeen years old.

Our courtship was a bit unorthodox. Without explaining why, Floyd convinced his sister-in-law, Rena, also my cousin, that she needed to visit her uncle Newby and Aunt Murtie Brown, my parents, and take him along. I wasn't home, so he had to sit there for about an hour and a half and listen to my dad describing just what he expected of any young man who wanted to date me, all the time being unaware of Floyd's intentions.

My friend, Joan Bean, and I had been in downtown Greensboro. Of course, we didn't have the luxury of a car, so we rode the city transit bus. Believe it or not, I had no reason to think that boy would be at my house when I got home. But, I was telling Joan how I would love to see a red Mercury town car in front of my house when I got there. To my surprise, and complete shock, as I turned the corner to my street, there it was sitting right in front of my house. I can't describe the feeling that came over me. To say the least, I was ecstatic!

To make a long story short, Floyd had convinced Rena that she should invite me to spend the night with her. Of course, she did. That night we had our first date. He took me to a square dance, of all things. It was just a little community thing, but I was overwhelmed because I had never done anything like that before in my very sheltered, Church-influenced existence.

That same night, there was a big fire out at the dairy farm. It just so happened that Floyd was a volunteer fireman. I had to go with him, because he wouldn't have had it any other way.

I sat in the car and watched as the big barn burned. Just then, I saw a familiar face in the crowd. It seems that the other man I had been dating for a little while, was a volunteer fireman too. Benny, the other guy, had even promised Floyd some beagle puppies. Needless to say, Floyd never got the puppies. I wonder if he ever thought he got the worst end of the deal! Ha Ha!

For a while, I juggled my relationships with Benny and with Floyd. I don't have to tell you that things got a bit upsetting to everyone involved. Even my dad got in on it! I don't think he was very happy with me, or the mess I had created.

It didn't take Floyd long to give me an ultimatum. He said it must be him, and only him, or else. At this point, I didn't know what I wanted, at least not until I told him I was not ready to commit to one person. To my utter dismay, I realized I had made a terrible mistake, but I was too stubborn to admit it. Sadly, we broke up for about nine months. During this time, Floyd made me sweat blood and regret my decision and my stubbornness. He would find out where I was going to be, then he would show up with the best-looking girl he could find.

## *Our Romance*

The year was 1952. Our church was having another Watch Night service. Floyd had brought a young lady to the service, and I was playing the piano as I usually did. Floyd was singing in the choir and Herb Snyder was sitting next to him. He asked Floyd what he would do for another chance with me. His response was, "She wouldn't date me now." Herb urged him to ask me and find out for sure. He did, and my heart almost exploded with joy! When I asked him what he would do about his date, he calmly replied, "I'll get someone else to take her home." And, he did.

We were engaged in May of 1952. Floyd had come to my house to take me to church. We practically lived at church, or at a singing somewhere. When I got into his car, he handed me a little box. He started to drive, but when I saw what it was, I told him he had to pull the car over and put it on my finger.

We finally arrived at the church, and it was all I could do to reign in my excitement and *not* show everyone my ring. Floyd and I were singing a duet that night, "I'm a Child of the King." One line in the song was, 'of rubies and diamonds, of silver and gold'. Mind you, I was playing the piano and singing at the same time, but I managed to hold up my ring hand and show everyone my diamond. It made quite a stir!

## My Song

Floyd loved music and singing better than anyone, other than my dad. The only problem was that when we first started dating, he could not carry a tune in a bucket with a lid. My dad and I would play the scales on the piano, but he just could not do it. He later told me that he wanted to sing so badly that he prayed to the Lord to give him a voice to sing with, and he would use it for God's glory. It was an amazing thing! God answered his prayer. Floyd still could not read a note of music, but I could play his part and he would sing it perfectly.

One Sunday afternoon, Floyd and I, along with Maurice and Elsie Butler, rode up to the mountains to take in the beautiful autumn leaves. While we were riding, we began to sing some gospel songs. We sounded pretty good, so we decided to bless the congregation at Gethsemane Baptist Church with our music. We were a hit! It became a regular thing for us to sing at our church.

Then, we began to attend homecomings at other churches in the afternoons, and sang there as well. Preachers would say, 'the quartet from the Gethsemane Baptist Church is here to sing for us'. Others began to invite us to sing for their church services. It wasn't long until we were asked to sing in gospel concerts. We sounded a little like the old Chuck Wagon Gang, but not on purpose.

In the meantime, Floyd and I were married on July 26, 1952. We continued to sing with the Butlers for about eight years. Elsie and Maurice began to be less interested in continuing with the quartet than Floyd and me.

By this time, our baby, Mark, had been born. It was getting to be quite a hassle for me to travel ten miles back and forth to church with a little baby. Floyd was on second shift at White Oak Mill.

We discussed the situation and decided that we needed to join a church closer to home. So, we joined Sixteenth Street Baptist Church. It was, at this time, that Floyd was approached, at his work place, by a man named Junior Poteat. He told Floyd that he had a daughter that could really sing, and he would like for us to come by and hear her.

*Our Group*

I'll never forget the scrawny, red-haired, sixteen-year-old who came into the room with a towel wrapped around her head; she was getting a home perm. She sat down at the piano and said, "Well, let's sing something." Her name was Jeanne Poteat.

We had already talked to a young man name Joe Vaugn Hill, who was a very good friend of Jeanne's. So, we began to practice, and it sounded pretty good. I would play the piano some of the time and Jeanne would play the others.

Everything was going great until Floyd and I decided to introduce Joe to my younger sister, Linda. It wasn't long until romance turned Joe's head, and heart, away from singing. Looking back on it now, I realize that it was all part of God's plan. Today, Joe and Linda have a wonderful family with two boys, Alan and David, and one girl, Sandra. So, I suppose we did a good thing after all.

Of course, since Joe and Linda were now married, we had to find a replacement singer for Joe. Floyd suggested that we get another young man named Bobby Grey Johnson. I had known Bob since we were kids, because we went to the same church, same school, and lived close to each other. I wasn't sure if he was the right fit for us, and Jeanne wasn't either. Granted, she didn't even know him, but she was just following my lead.

Bob began to sing with us around 1960 or 1961. I remember this because Mark was born March 7, 1958, and he was about two years old at the time. Bob had only been with us about eight months when he and Jeanne announced their engagement. Talk about a turnaround!

Things were going very well, then Floyd decided that we needed a full-time piano player. Earl Brewer, who I had gone to school with, and lived a short distance from us, was a self-taught musician and a really good one. We asked him if he was interested in being our piano man and he gladly agreed. This decision was one of the best ones we ever made. Earl knew just what we needed, and he brought a definite touch of professionalism to the group.

We had so much fun when we met together to practice on Tuesday and Thursday nights. Before we met each night, Earl would have already worked out our song arrangements, so all we had to do was to learn our parts. But, we all still had a say in the arrangements, and it all seemed to just... work.

This was when we started doing the big-time concerts. We went everywhere and sang with all the top groups at the time. We did concerts with groups like the Speer Family, the Blackwood Brothers, Wendy Bagwell and the Sunlighters, the Chuck Wagon Gang, the Stamps, the Oakridge Boys, the Rambos, the LeFevres, the Cathedrals, and many others. We even sang at the Cathedral of Tomorrow when Bro. Rex Humbard was there. It was a huge auditorium; so big that you could fit a baseball field in it.

On one of our trips to the Cathedral, we had a new bus driver named Burt Lancaster. No, he was not the infamous actor from the movies. Burt, our Burt, was a long-distance truck driver for a local company on Greensboro. And, since we had just bought a new bus to travel in, and none of our guys had any experience in driving such a large vehicle, Burt agreed to drive for us and teach Floyd how to drive.

It was on this trip that we were learning a new song entitled, "From Now on, I'll Trust in Jesus." We were singing it on the bus as we were traveling to the

Cathedral of Tomorrow. As we sang, Burt began to cry. We all assumed they were tears of joy, so we sang it again. Then, Burt would cry again. We sang it on Sunday morning and it seemed that the Lord really came down among us. That night, in the evening service, Bro. Rex asked us to sing it again. People began to flood the altar and we suddenly saw Burt, nearly running toward the front of the church, weeping. His wife, Gay, was seated in the audience, on the left, and she joined him at the altar. Burt was gloriously saved that night. Praise the Lord! And, Gay rededicated her life to the Christ. It was then that we realized Burt's tears had been of conviction, not of rejoicing. But, I can assure you that there were tears of rejoicing that night on the way back home.

There were many occasions, when we were with the Statesmen Quartet at a concert, that Big Jim, their bass singer, would take us backstage and give is a manuscript of a new song, or songs, he had written for us to sing. We recorded several of them.

Hovie Lister, manager of the Statesmen, was also a preacher at a small church in Georgia. We sang there several times. Sometimes, while we were singing, Hovie would either sing with us, or he would push Earl off the piano bench and play along with us.

Then, there was the time we were singing in Lakeland, Florida. All the groups of singers were there! Back then, when you claimed to be at an all-night singing, that was exactly how long you were there... all night!

We had had our bus a short while and the Kingsmen had just gotten theirs. It was a newer model than ours, so they kept teasing us, claiming that their bus was better than ours. Later, on our way home, we had only gone a short way, when we spotted someone in the middle of the road, on his knees, waving his arms. As we slowed to a stop, we noticed that it was Big Jim Hammel of the Kingsmen Quartet. Their "new" bus had broken down. Imagine that!

Good ol' Floyd, being the great guy he was, told all the Kingsmen to climb onto our bus, because they were due to sing at the Reynolds auditorium that night. Our friend, Burt, was driving our bus, so Floyd stayed with the Kingsmen bus, got it repaired and running, and brought it to them that night. What great memories!

Our very first group!

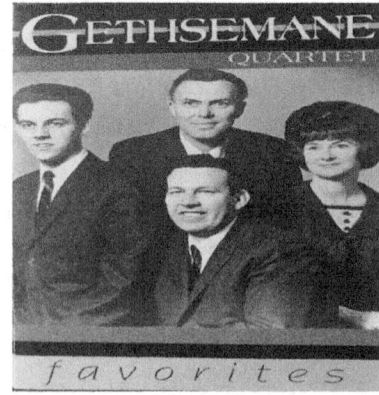

And, here are a few more pictures of us over the many years.

26

# Chapter Three
*The Bus*

Before we got our first bus, we traveled in a nine-passenger Cadillac. I'll never forget those trips! We had to haul our clothes and our product in a U-Haul trailer behind us. We had to stop periodically and rehang our clothes because they would be in a crumpled mess on the floor of the trailer. Since a lot of our traveling was done at night, we had to find time to sleep. So, some of us would sleep in the seats while others would find space in the floor. These were not some of my happier memories. Sometimes, we would pretend we were coming from a funeral, crying and wiping our eyes with handkerchiefs. We got a lot of strange looks. Ha! Ha!

I think we were the third group, at the time, to purchase a bus. And, we wouldn't even have bought one if Earl hadn't convinced Floyd that we needed one. When he went shopping for one, Floyd went to Winston Salem. He told the salesman what he wanted, and the man was amused. He had never heard of anyone buying a bus for personal use. He showed Floyd what he had available, but Floyd didn't see anything that he liked. However, when he was getting ready to leave, he saw a bus pulling into the lot. Floyd told the man, "That's it! That's the one I want." Unfortunately, the man claimed that it wasn't for sale. Floyd answered, "Let me know when it is."

An amazing thing happened after that. Floyd got a call a few days later informing him that they would sell him the bus he wanted. But now, we had a problem; how we would pay for it. Floyd went to the bank and saw the manager, explaining why he needed the money. The bank manager could not believe what he was hearing. He had never financed the purchase of a bus for an individual. At the time, Jim Melvin was the head of that particular bank. So, Floyd wrote him a letter, asking for his assistance in getting a loan to buy the bus. Mr. Melvin made it possible for us to get our bus. Later, Mr. Melvin became the mayor of Greensboro, and Floyd never forgot the man's kindness.

After we got the bus, traveling became so much easier and much more pleasant. Floyd said once, a man he worked with asked him if the bus was big enough for the four of us to travel in. He replied, "Well, the Lord wanted us to have a train, but there aren't tracks everywhere we go." Needless to say, that retort put the man in his place.

It sure made a difference to have plenty of space to move around in and not be so cramped, even though it only had eight seats and a driver's seat. The back of it was filled with beds and closet space. Sadly, it didn't have a toilet in it. Which reminds me of an incident that happened on our way home one Sunday night from Ohio.

### *The Shenanigans*

Everyone was asleep except Floyd and Earl Brewer. Earl was our piano player at the time, and a really good one. Jeanne Johnson, her husband, Bob, and I were in our bunks, asleep. Earl had been driving for about three hours and decided to stop at a little service station in Hillsville, Virginia. He needed a bathroom break and a cup of coffee. When I woke up, the bus was stopped, so I got off without telling anyone because they were asleep. I found the ladies restroom, which was outside the service station, like they all were back then. When I was about to leave, I heard the bus motor fire up. Panicked, I ran out of the restroom just in time to see the bus going down the road. I cannot begin to describe how I felt!

It was about two o'clock in the morning, snowing, and cold as the North Pole. This was in the early 60's and I had really big hair; big, teased-up hair. To protect all this big hair, I had wrapped it in toilet paper and tied a silk scarf around it. I had on pajamas, bedroom slippers and house robe, and of course, I had a coat over all that. Can you imagine what a sight I must have been chasing the bus and screaming, "No, Honey! No!?" I know, now, that I should have saved my breath because no one could have heard me over that loud bus motor.

From our stopping point, it would have taken them two hours to reach home and find out I was missing. Then, when they finally discovered it, it would take them two more hours to come back for me. All I could think was that I was going to have to wait for them for four hours! I cried and cried until I had the snubs. Ha! Ha!

Then, I spotted a police car coming toward me. I can't imagine what the man must have been thinking as he slowly approached me. When they pulled up even with me, I tried to explain that the bus had left me behind. They were confused because they had no idea that a bus even ran through there at that time of night. And, who would even be traveling on a bus, dressed, or undressed, as I was?

Thank the good Lord that they had mercy on me. After I explained that it was the Gethsemane Quartet bus that I was talking about, I slid into the front seat of the patrol car. They assured me that they could catch up to the bus, and they did. About fifteen miles down the road, the patrol car, with me tucked inside, pulled the bus over. Floyd was driving, and he couldn't understand why he was being pulled over. He asked Earl if he'd been speeding and Earl reassured him that he hadn't. Floyd was shutting everything down and didn't even have a chance to open the door before I began banging on it. When he opened it, I stood there in my pajamas and big hair and he couldn't believe what he was seeing. It was the shock of his life! In fact, he told me later that he thought it must have been my twin standing there because he just knew that I was sound asleep in my bunk.

Of course, by this time, everyone on the bus was awake. And, though they thought the whole fiasco was hilarious, I admit that I did not share in their mirth. I wish I could tell you that such a thing never happened again, but I can't.

We had been singing in a revival in Reidsville for a week and it was Saturday night. Since we were scheduled to sing in Altavista, Virginia the next morning, we all agreed to drive there and spend the night in the church parking lot. That way, we knew we would be on time for the Sunday services.

Floyd had a problem with bleeding ulcers and it was very painful, but sometimes, a milkshake would help soothe the pain. Since Floyd was driving, as soon as he spotted the Dairy Queen, he pulled into the parking lot and stopped right in front of a laundromat. He was the only one awake, since we were driving at night, so he walked up to the Dairy Queen alone. I woke up and looked outside. Seeing the laundromat, I assumed that's where Floyd had gone. So, I hopped off the bus and went in search of a restroom.

Meanwhile, Floyd found that the Dairy Queen was closed and returning to the bus, he started driving away. After a while of searching the laundromat, and finding no one, I decided to get back on the bus. Imagine my dismay to find the thing missing. Again!

This time, however, I knew the bus's destination. So, I walked up to the Dairy Queen, hoping to use their phone to call the pastor of the church in Altavista. Remember the wardrobe from the previous story? Instant replay! As I walked up to the Dairy Queen, which was now opened, the customers and staff had no idea what to think. I asked to use the phone and they reluctantly agreed. Then, to add insult to injury, I found that the phone was a payphone and I had no money with me! So, I had to ask for a dime to make the call. Imagine my embarrassment!

While I was attempting to make my phone call, Floyd had already discovered that I wasn't in my bunk and had turned around to come back for me. (That's how long I was in the laundromat!) He'd already pulled into the church's parking lot and went back to his own bunk to get some sleep, when he realized I wasn't in mine. He thought I might have been playing a trick on him, so he searched all the bunks and closets, looking for places I could hide. When he realized what must have happened, he high-tailed it back to find me. When he found me, I was making that phone call and we were both so relieved!

Sometime later, we were singing in Hampton, Virginia on a Sunday morning. Mark was just a small boy and he made friends everywhere we went. Often, this would create a problem for us, because we would be ready to leave, and he was nowhere to be found.

That Sunday morning, his father warned him, he had to be ready to leave when we were, because we had another concert that night at a different place and we only had a short time to get there. As usual, we were all set to leave, and... no Mark. Floyd said, "I'm going to have to break him of this." So, he started the bus and we pretended that we were leaving. Immediately, we saw Mark come running around the side of the church, crying. He got on the bus and jumped up into my lap.

"Honey, you know your daddy wouldn't leave you," I claimed.

To this Mark replied, "Oh yes, Mommy! If he would leave you, I know he would leave me."

I think we both learned our lessons. We never got left again.

# Chapter Four
*Our Work*

Floyd and I worked secular jobs as well as keeping our concert dates. I worked for A.T.&T. and Floyd, for a steel fabricating company, called Edgecomb Steel. We would sometimes sing twenty-eight nights out of a month while still working our jobs during the day. I wonder, now, how we managed to do it then. It had to be the grace of God, along with the fact that we were young. When we were singing far away and had to make long trips, we would use our vacation days from work. Somehow, we managed to keep the two separated.

One of the men who sang with us in the early 80's explained it like this: our music ministry was our full-time job, and our secular jobs were only part-time. I think he had it just about right.

*Our Choice*

It didn't take Floyd and I long to realize that the "concert scene" wasn't exactly where the Lord wanted us to be.

Back in the early days of the Quartet Convention, they were just beginning to lay down some ground rules. One of the rules stated that if you were a member of the Convention, you shouldn't do so many church dates. Floyd was in one of those early meetings when this was proposed. He walked away from that meeting disappointed because he knew that we couldn't do that. God had other plans for us. So, we separated ourselves from the Convention, and we have never been sorry. Of course, we remained friends with many of the groups who did stay.

But, God knew His plans for us. Soon, churches began to open their doors to us, and we were reassured that we were in the will of God.

One day, Floyd got a call from Brock Speer of the Speer family. His parents were getting older and finding it more and more demanding to keep up with the pace of being on the road for days, or weeks, at a time. Since they were ready to retire, Brock needed to find a replacement for them. He asked me to replace his mom and Floyd to replace his dad.

Now, Brock's dad sang tenor, but Floyd sang bass. However, Brock assured Floyd that he could teach him to sing the tenor part. Plus, Brock knew that Floyd was a good bus driver and maintenance man. As honored as we were to be asked, and we relayed this message to Brock, we knew that we were right where God wanted us to be. Also, we had Mark, who was about six, and if we joined the Speer family, we would have to leave him for extended periods of time. We weren't ready to do that. We never regretted our decision to obey God.

Brock, then, asked Floyd if he knew of anyone who could fill in for his parents and he gave them Jeanne

Johnson's name. Jeanne and Bob traveled with the Speer family for almost ten years and did a wonderful job. Jeanne was even voted 'Miss Gospel Music' once. There is no doubt that she was meant to fill that position.

After Jeanne and Bob left, we continued with Earl Brewer singing and playing the piano. Then, a young man from Danville, Virginia, named Wayne Hilliard, joined us.

Later, when Wayne left, and Earl's health caused him to slow down for a while, we found ourselves in need of someone to replace them.

We heard about a young man in Winston Salem, named Darius Stewart, a most unusual person. I don't think I ever met anyone who was a more devoted Christian than him. So, we hired him.

Along with Darius, came his friend, Buddy Brady, who was as opposite in personality from Darius as two people can be. But, they were the best of friends. Buddy could play the piano and the guitar, and he had a good philosophy about life: yesterday is gone, so forget it; tomorrow's not here yet, so don't sweat it; if I can get through today, I'm a happy camper.

We had a lot of fun with these two! The old saying, "opposites attract" was certainly true for these men. And, no jab intended, but Darius was a genius and they really complimented each other. Ha! Ha!

## *Our Adventures*

I remember one day, while riding on the bus, we passed a dead animal in the road. Immediately, Darius and Buddy began to sing, "O, possum, O, possum, how do you feel with your guts lying there in the road?" I'm not quite sure if they came up with that in the moment or if it had been rehearsed before. Either way, I don't believe their song would've gotten very far on the Hit Parade.

Darius was one of the most spiritual young men that I had ever met. He was truly genuine. He was continuously coming up with, what we would call, 'golden nuggets' that the Lord had given him. Everywhere we went, pastors would ask him to share some of these precious thoughts with the congregation. And, on occasion, they would even ask him to preach. Though he never claimed to be a God-called preacher, he still made a good one. He loved to teach and share what God had opened up to him.

We had some wonderful times with these two, and some unpredictable times. Buddy would fall asleep at the most unusual times.

Once, while we were traveling to Tennessee for a meeting, Floyd asked Buddy to do the driving since he'd worked all week in the steel company and he'd driven the day before. Buddy agreed and took the wheel so the rest of us could get some sleep. That night, there was a terrible storm. The rain and thunder were so loud that it woke me out of a dead sleep! It took me a good while to get back to sleep.

The next morning, as we gathered around the breakfast table at a restaurant close to the church where we would sing, Floyd asked Buddy how long the storm had lasted. Confused, Buddy replied, "What storm?" Believe me, that was a bit unnerving.

Another time, we were on our way to Charlotte, North Carolina, and Floyd asked Buddy to drive again, giving him specific directions to our destination. Buddy took the wheel and the rest of us went to bed. During the night, the bus did a few lunges from side to side, then came to a complete stop.

We awoke to realize that Buddy had taken I-85 toward Raleigh instead of toward Charlotte. It took us the rest of the night to make it to our destination, but it should have only taken us a few hours. After this, Floyd was a little more selective of the times he allowed Buddy to drive. Ha!

Another man also joined the group when Buddy and Darius were with us. His name was Bill Brooks. The three of them had been friends for quite a while even before coming to the Gethsemane Quartet.

# Chapter Five
*Our Friends*

During these years with Buddy, Darius, and Bill, the quartet was privileged to sing for some of God's choicest servants. We got well acquainted with Dr. Jerry Falwell back in the late 1960's, and sang for him at Thomas Road Baptist Church every two or three months. This was the only church we sang in where you had to arrive thirty to forty-five minutes before the service in order to get in line to get inside. Bro. Jerry ate many meals at our house. He would stop over on his way home from a meeting with three to five people with him. What a great memory of a great man!

We sang at Thomas Road for many Pastor's conferences with well-known preachers such as Dr. B.R. Lakin, who became a very dear friend, Dr. John Rawlings, Dr. Bob Gray, and Bro. Lester Roloff, Dr. John R. Rice, Dr. Bobby Roberson, and Dr. Curtis Hutson, just to name a few.

Bro. Lester Roloff was a very unique man. He had several homes for wayward girls, boys, men, and women. The main one was in Corpus Christie, Texas. It was called 'The Rebecca Home for Girls'. There were girls that were pregnant out of wedlock, addicted to alcohol or dope, or just delinquent or uncontrollable at home.

Bro Roloff would have us down at least once a year, for a week each time. Sometimes, he would fly us down, and other times, we would drive the bus. While there, we would minister to several of the other homes. He would fly us to the other homes' locations in his plane.

Once, he flew us over the King Ranch! He flew so low that we skimmed the tree tops, causing the antelopes and other wild animals to scurry out from under the trees, frightened.

He cooked our meals, or helped cook them. All their food was organically grown on their farm, and the fish was caught in the Inner-Coastal Canal. Even the goats milk was delicious.

Once, he sent a Lear jet, that belonged to a very famous man, Red Adair, to pick us up at PTI airport. Red Adair was the man who was famous for putting out big oil fires.

We would also do rally meetings with Dr. Falwell before his college grew too large. He was a true friend and, together, we created many wonderful memories.

I remember, once, when we were singing with the Griffiths, and their son, Matthew was about six years old. We sang at Thomas Road that morning. I bought Matthew a new three-piece suit and a pair of penny loafers. He looked so proud! He asked me, before the service, if I thought Dr. Falwell would notice his shoes.

"Of course, he will," I declared. "How could he not notice something so fine?"

After the service, Dr. Falwell took us all out to lunch and I managed to pull him over to the side and tell him what Matthew had wondered. When we were gathered 'round the lunch table, Bro. Jerry looked at Matthew and said, "Matthew, those are really great shoes you have on."

Matthew's eyes were as big as saucers! He looked at me and said excitedly, "He did notice my shoes! He really did!" This made a tremendous impression on this young fella.

*Our Changes*

When Buddy Brady decided to leave, we tried out several replacements. There was a young man named, Winfred Way, who had a ton of talent. He was only with us a short while.

Then, there was Von Hohn. I will never forget the first time he came to our house to audition. He drove up in a yellow Corvette and dressed to the nines! He walked through the door with a big smile on his face, sat down in a rocking chair in our den, and began to rock away. He was such a friendly, young man and could really play that piano. He was with us for six or seven years, off and on.

Our son, Mark, had sung with us since he was eleven years old. Now, as a young man, graduating from High School, he was headed off to Bob Jones University in Greenville, South Carolina. So, now we had to find someone to take his place.

At this time, the group consisted of Floyd, myself, Mark, and a beautiful, young girl named Janice Swanger. Also, for a short time, Kay Pascal sang with us, and of course, Von Hohn played the piano. Sadly, Janice died in a car accident at only twenty-three years old. What a tragedy!

*Our Convictions*

While working at Western Electric, which would later become known as A.T.&T. I met a lady named Sylvia Cox. She was married to James Cox, who I'd known for years. We even dated on occasion, but we were only destined to be good friends. James and Sylvia had a son about the same age as Mark, named Alan. When Alan found out that Mark would be leaving the group to go to college, he called Floyd and asked him if he could audition to take Mark's place. He agreed and asked Alan to come on over for a try-out. I'll never forget the way he looked when he walked in the door. He had on a leather jacket and boots, his hair was down past his shoulders and he rode in on a motorcycle.

Now, there had been some controversy over whether, or not, a man should have long hair. It had been our policy that our men-singers would have short hair, because Floyd was very particular about how we presented ourselves. He never wanted to offend. However, Floyd didn't mention anything to Alan about his hair.

We sang a while and when we were finished practicing that night, we were about to say goodnight, when Alan looked to Floyd and said, "I know I've got to get my hair cut, Floyd. Don't worry, I will."

We were scheduled to leave for Kansas City the next weekend to sing, and I was concerned about Alan's hair. I asked Floyd, "What are we going to do, Honey, if he shows up next week and his hair is too long?"

Floyd, in his typical way, stated, "Well, then he will just not go."

The next week came around and when Alan walked through our kitchen door, his head, above his ears, was almost completely shaved. Oh, me of little faith! Ha! Ha!

Alan was married to a precious, young girl named, Melody. She was the daughter of Rev. Marcus Sizemore, who had also sung with us for a year or so. Since they were newlyweds, she traveled with us, too. Now, we had four young people traveling with us and we had so much fun. I believe they helped us stay young, as well.
Alan went on to pastor several churches in Virginia and Oklahoma. His church was one that fed the

people of Oklahoma City after the tornadoes twisted through their town.

Later, he pastored Green St. Baptist Church in High Point. Presently, he is on the board of Piedmont Baptist Bible College in Winston Salem and pastoring the Journey Church.

Then, came Jean Pollard, a young lady from Danville, Virginia, along with her husband, Donnie. Jean was an amazing pianist, and played with us for several years. She has gone on to minister in several churches, teaching piano, and working in the church orchestra.

There was also a young man named Livingston Freeman, or Livvy, for short. He filled in for Jean while she was on maternity leave. Livvy was a masterful pianist!

## *Our Cautionary Tales*

We've made so many memories throughout the years. Once, we were traveling through the mountains of Virginia at night. Everyone was sleeping except the driver, Floyd. There was a warning device on the motor that would go off if anything went wrong, giving us mere seconds to pull off the road.

Well, late that night, the buzzer sounded, and Floyd pulled off the road to check the motor and determine the problem. He found out that we had been losing water. Of course, by this time, we were all wide awake and trying to determine what we should do. There were no houses or any signs of life nearby, and we had to have water, or the bus would be going nowhere.

So, we did what we always did when a problem arose... we prayed. After we finished our prayer, Von Hohn exclaimed, "Do you hear that?" Of course, we all quietened and listened. The fellows followed the sound and found a very small stream of water along the side of the road. We had a shouting good time!

Another time was when Alan found a shortcut on Highway 16. We were well into the trip when the road began to narrow... and narrow... and narrow. It became so narrow that if another car had approached us, we wouldn't have been able to share the road, and there was no way to turn around or go back. Then, we saw a sign that read, "No Vehicles Over 30 Feet Allowed." That was just great! Our bus was at least 35 feet long! Since there was no way around it, we had to keep going.

Floyd also told us there were times when he was driving around a curve and couldn't see the road below him when he looked out the window.

As if that wasn't enough, we came to the reason for the sign...a cable bridge. Our bus weighed at least 23,000 pounds. How were we going to cross that bridge? First, Floyd asked everyone to get off the bus. We did, then we watched as my brave husband attempted to take the bus across the bridge. God protected him; no question about it. It also helped that the bus was longer than the bridge and the full weight of the bus was never completely on the bridge at one time.

Another memorable occasion occurred one summer when Mark was home from college and already married. He and his lovely bride, Cindy, were traveling with us along with Robert and Patti Griffith and their two children, Matthew and Audra. This time, we were in South Carolina.

After singing at a church on Saturday night, we were on our way to another singing for Sunday morning, somewhere in Hartsville. It was after midnight when we arrived at the church and the pastor was waiting for us. The pastor told Floyd to park the bus around the back of the church in the grass. Suspicious about this, Floyd asked the man if he knew where the septic tank was to be sure the bus would be safe. The pastor said it would be fine, so Floyd parked the bus as he was directed, and we all settled in our bunks for the night.

When we woke up on Sunday morning, we realized that the bus was strangely leaning. We investigated and realized the bus had sank into their septic tank. Needless to say, Floyd was not a happy camper. The pastor said not to worry because there was a man in the church that had some heavy machinery to pull it out. Of course, Floyd was worried about there being something wrong with the bus, but when they pulled it out, we found that there was no damage done. Thank God!

A little while later, Robert, Mark, and Floyd were getting our sound system out along with our recordings. At one point, Floyd looked up and saw Robert and Mark with a large "Voice of Theatre" speaker hoisted above their heads, coming down a narrow hallway. When he saw this, he cautioned them not to go that way because it was too dangerous. But, they didn't listen. When he looked up again, they were doing the same thing and coming down the same narrow hallway.

When Mark tripped, and fell, the huge speaker with a large metal horn on the front, fell also. The horn cut Mark on the neck and knocked him senseless for a few minutes. We called for an ambulance, but when Floyd saw what had happened to his son, it upset him so much that he needed to go out for some air. However, as he headed for the front door, he passed out at the back of the church. I began running from the front of the church, to take care of Mark, to the back, to take care of Floyd.

We were able to carry on with the service, at least with those of us that were left, but the excitement was just beginning. An elderly woman on her way into the service, fell and cracked her head on the sidewalk. She was sent to the hospital and we were later informed that she had passed away.
After the service, Floyd told the pastor to do us a favor and never call on us to sing again. And, he didn't.

Mark and Cindy sang with us for several years after they were married. At this same time, the Griffiths were traveling with us. They were with us for about eight and a half years. It was during this time that Rob wrote some of his best songs: "God Himself the Lamb", "Under His Feet", "The Shepherd," and so many more. We had some wonderful times together, including making six recordings. Mark and Cindy joined us for three of them.

After the Griffiths went out on their own, we recalled a young man who had been with us before, Von Hohn. By this time, he had married a lovely young lady named, Teressa. They sang with us for a while until their family began to grow, requiring more of their time at home. We realized that we needed to find some replacements for them and Mark pointed us in the direction of a wonderful couple from their church. Their names were Greg and Kathy Ottoway. Greg was a very good singer/songwriter and played the piano. They were with us until 1994 when we decided to retire. They did a wonderful job and we are all still friends who stay in touch. They are a part of our extended family.

# Chapter Six
*Our Precious Gift*

Going back a little bit, when Floyd and I had been married for about six years, we both wanted children, but it just wasn't happening for us. I can't begin to describe how badly I wanted to be a mother. We figured, after so many years of marriage, and no positive results, that something must be wrong with one or both of us. After many doctor visits and a couple of surgeries, we were informed that I had a bad case of endometriosis. Of course, they told us that anything was possible, but it was highly unlikely that I would ever get pregnant.

I was devastated beyond words, but we kept praying. About six months later, we went on vacation with some friends. I felt great before we left, but as we sat down to breakfast and everyone started ordering, I realized that just the thought of food made me cringe. When it came my turn to order, I felt all I could stomach was some buttermilk with salt in it. This was about all I could tolerate the whole trip.

I waited until we returned home to go to the doctor. It didn't take him long to realize that I was pregnant. Thrilled beyond measure, I called Floyd and he shared in my joy.

God was gracious to me in allowing me to conceive when even the doctors said it was most likely impossible. My pregnancy was unreal! The worst thing that I had to endure was a few weeks of nausea. When I got over that phase, I could *not* have felt better. I had no swelling of the legs, no blood pressure issues, really no issues at all.

I weighed ninety-eight pounds when I got pregnant. And, after gaining close to fifty pounds, I lost it all three months after I delivered. I had a natural child birth, although that isn't what we'd planned to do. And, from the beginning of my first labor pain to the final birth, only an hour and a half had passed. Floyd said he felt cheated because he didn't even get to pace the floor. Ha! Ha! In fact, he had just stepped off the elevator when he heard the doctor ask, "Where is Andrews?" The doctor was holding Mark in his arms.

He watched as the doctor held the baby by his feet to measure him, and since he didn't exactly know what was happening, he told the man, "Be careful! That's my boy you have there!"

We named our baby boy, Ted Mark Andrews. The name, 'Ted', came from another young man that we were very fond of, and the name, 'Mark', was a Biblical name that we both liked.

He was always a happy child. I remember, once, when I was showing off some of his pictures at work, my supervisor made a comment about him. He said, "He looks like a happy child, and I predict he will always be a happy person." Truer words were never spoken. When Mark was two years old, we learned he had a hernia and was going to have to have surgery. I will never forget how I felt as I watched his little body sitting in the middle of the gurney, waving his little hand, and being wheeled through the emergency room doors. Floyd and I were basket-cases. The doctor told us to go somewhere and have a meal, and Mark would be okay when we got back. We did as he asked, but neither of us ate much at all. Six months later, he had to have a hernia on the other side fixed as well. Since Floyd and I worked secular jobs five days a week and then had a music ministry that occupied our weekends and many of our week nights, Mark had to go to Baines Nursery School each morning. His dad would take him to school on his way to work.

Once, when Floyd had to pick him up from school, he walked in to find Mark being punished, standing in the corner. His teacher told Floyd that Mark had hit another teacher on the behind. On the way home, he asked Mark why he would do such a thing. Mark innocently replied, "It just looked like it would hit good."

This wasn't the only incident in which he was involved at the nursery. One day when Floyd picked him up, again, one of the teachers told him about an incident that had happened that day. One of the other boys had broken his toy and was crying. Mark put his arms around the boy and said, "Don't cry. My daddy will buy you a new one." Even as young as he was, he had such a big heart and he realized his daddy's generosity.

At four years old, Mark came home from school with an ugly blister in the palm of his hand. I asked him how he got it and he said it was from the acting bars at school. I warned him to stay off them until the wound had properly healed, but he didn't listen. The next day, he was back on the bars and soon, the school called us to come pick him up because his hand didn't look very good. Floyd quickly took him to see Dr. Roy Smith, his pediatrician. Mark had red streaks running up his arm, so they operated immediately. He stayed in the hospital for seven days. It seemed that his appetite wasn't affected, though. He would eat his food, and everyone else's too.

At six years old, he and his good friend, Johnny Dwyer, were out riding their bikes. Floyd was over at the new property we'd purchased, and I was home alone. After a while, I only saw Johnny riding in our yard and asked him where Mark was. He replied, "I think Mark needs you."

I looked up and saw Mark walking slowly up the road to our house holding his right arm. His arm was crooked at a strange angle. I ran to him and he was crying. He said, "Please, pray for me, Mama." He had fallen out of a tree and broken his right arm just a few weeks before he was going to enter the first grade.

Who would have thought that a broken arm could be life-threatening? Well, it so happened that while Mark was in surgery, repairing his arm, he had regurgitated and began choking and turning blue. Unbeknownst to me, Mark had eaten some peanuts before the surgery and I wasn't able to tell the doctor that because I hadn't known. When the surgery was over, they came out and told me to go in and comfort him. Imagine my dismay when I saw splats of blood on his shirt. The nurse explained how he'd choked and that she had to dig the peanuts out of his throat with her fingers. He was in the hospital for a week to make sure he didn't take pneumonia. Thank God, he didn't!

During Mark's second year at Bob Jones University, he was no longer traveling with the quartet. This particular weekend, we were on our way to sing in Elizabeth City, North Carolina. As usual, we were all sitting in the front of the bus, laughing and talking, when suddenly, it was as if the weight of the whole world fell on my heart. I knew I needed to pray.

Without saying anything to the others, I got up and headed to the back room on the bus where I began to pray. I prayed for all the needs that God brought to my mind, especially for Mark. I prayed until the burden was lifted, then went back up front with the others.

When we arrived at the church, Floyd, Alan, and Von began to take the sound system inside. Unaware of what was going on in the church, the girls and I began getting dressed for the service. Alan came onto the bus and told me that Floyd wanted me to come into the church right away.

When I got inside, I found the police there, and Floyd talking on the phone. He had written a note and left it on the desk, which read, "Son in accident."

It turns out, Mark had an accident while playing soccer at Bob Jones, and was in surgery, in critical condition. His kidney had been ruptured by a blow to his side. It was a life or death situation, but by the grace of God, he survived.

We traveled all night from Elizabeth City to Greenville, South Carolina, stopping in Greensboro long enough to pick up Cindy, his girlfriend at the time.

Mark spent several weeks recovering. The university was so wonderful to him, and to us, during that time. Through it all, God gave him the sweetest peace; that peace that passes all understanding. He did recover, and though he has only one kidney, he has done amazingly well.

There were several other incidents along the way, but nothing really major until he graduated from college. He had an interview in Altavista for a job. He ate a big breakfast that morning, then took off for Virginia. I went to work, like I usually did, at the Guilford Center, working for A.T.&T. When I came home that evening, I went to Mark's room and lay across his bed, something I never do. After a while, I heard Mark come home through the kitchen door, walk down the hall to his room, and speak to me while leaning against his dresser. He explained, "Dad didn't want me to tell you this until you could see that I'm okay. I had a wreck on the way to Altavista this morning. I rolled my car a few times, but I'm all right."

Of course, I had mixed emotions, but I was happy to see that he was okay. But, at the same time, I could only imagine what could have been.

If I could have sat down and wrote down all the things I could ever want in a son, I couldn't have pictured a more wonderful son. Mark has always been an obedient, honorable son. Of course, we had some growing pains along the way, but nothing major. He was trustworthy as a boy, and still is, as a man. He is a man of integrity, a Godly man. He loves his wife, his family, and his parents. He has always honored us and, according to the word of God, he will be rewarded as it is the first commandment with promise. He is a faithful church member and a deacon. He also teaches a series of classes on creation versus evolution, apologetics, and the Jews return to Israel. He and his partner, Jo Smith, have a business of their own, Better Care Wellness Consultants.

Most of all, he has been true to his promise to me. When His father passed away on August 2, 2004, Mark told me that he would be there for me, and he has been. I love him dearly.

Me & my son, Mark

# Chapter Seven
## *Our Blessings*

Mark graduated from Bob Jones University in 1980. He had been courting a beautiful, young lady named, Cindy Trantham for about four or five years. They had started dating in high school and continued through college.

After graduation, Mark asked Cindy to marry him, but she still had another year to go at the University of North Carolina. However, her parents had told her that they would still finance her last year of college even if they married. So, with both of their parents' blessing, they were married on July 19, 1980.

At this time, I was employed at A.T.&T. at the Guilford Center. My supervisor became very interested in Mark and what he was doing. He asked if Mark had found a job yet and I told him that he hadn't, but he surely needed one. When he asked about Mark's major in college, I informed him that he was an accounting major.

Unfortunately, at this time, A.T.&T. wasn't hiring because the company was being split into three entities. So, I was very surprised when my supervisor told me to have Mark come in and fill out a job request form. I, of course, passed the information on to Mark that very night.

The following day, a Thursday, at three o'clock in the afternoon, I was busy working, when a department head called me, asking to see me. Since he was in the professional side of the Guilford Center, I tried to describe to him how he could make his way to me. Instead, he said, "Never mind. Just come down to the main entrance. I have someone who wants to see you." So, off I went to the main entrance.

When I got down there, I saw this gentleman standing with Mark. It seems they had called him to come in for an interview and was so impressed with his appearance and his behavior that the man hired him on the spot. That's how Mark came to work for ASA, later to be known as AON. He worked there for twenty-eight years.

He and Cindy rented an apartment in Burlington, so they would be half way between Mark's job, in Greensboro, and Cindy's classes, at UNC Chapel Hill.

It was nine years later when our little Madison Whitney Andrews was born, on January 12, 1989. I remember that I had almost given up on being a grandmother, but believe me, she was worth the wait.

Fifteen months after that, Miss Chelsea Nichole Andrews made her debut. I remember thinking, before she was born, I couldn't possibly love another child as much as Madison. Boy, was I wrong! As soon as they put that little red-headed girl in my arms, I found I had more love in my heart than I realized.

I started keeping Madison when she was very young because Cindy worked at Wesley Long Hospital and had to be at work early in the morning. And, Mark had to be at work at eight o'clock, so I began keeping both girls at least two or three days and nights a week. What a joy these girls were to me! When they would go home, I could hardly wait until they would be back with me. I was in my sixties then, and when they'd leave I would be worn out. But, I was happy and anxious to have them come back.

We had so much fun together! The girls would expect me to do everything that they did. We played all over the house, putting up tents, using blankets and sheets. After the girls could read, we would put signs all over the house, and I would be their personal taxi. They were so busy and there was somewhere to go every day.

Mark and Cindy brought them over about bedtime, Mark told his dad that he'd had to spank Chelsea before the got there. As I was tucking them into bed, Chelsea slipped her arms around my neck and said, "My daddy whooped me tonight." I asked her why he had to do that, and she claimed it was for messing with Madison.

I told her that she needed to leave Madison alone when she says she's had enough. Chelsea said, "Mee Maw, it's just my mind. When my mind is on this side, (pointing to her right temple) I do berry good things. When my mind is on this side, (pointing to her left temple) I do berry bad things. When my mind is right here, (pointing to the middle of her forehead) I do berry, berry good things." Then, in dismay, she said, "Mee Maw, sometimes my mind just makes me crazy." Ha! Ha! I will never forget that! I still laugh about it today.

One night, when Madison was barely three-years-old, I was holding and rocking her. We were talking about Heaven and she asked where Heaven was. I thought a moment, then replied, "I'm not sure where Heaven is, but wherever Jesus is, that's where Heaven is." Then, I added, "And, you know what? Jesus lives in my heart, and one day, you will ask Jesus to live in your heart."

She quickly replied, "Mee Maw, Jesus already lives in my heart!" How precious!

I slept with the girls on either side of me, and we would take turns praying. They would always pray for a good man to marry! One night, I suggested a change in their prayer for a 'good man'. I told them that one day, they might find a good man that wasn't a godly man. That night, when it was Chelsea's turn to pray, she prayed for a good and godly man, emphasizing the word 'godly'. God heard those sweet and honest prayers and gave them both good and godly men!

Once, I was encouraging Madison to eat a little bit more food. She said, "If I eat another bite, I'm gonna blow out!" She had overheard us adults say that if we ate another bite, we would explode. She had the basic idea.

Mark and Cindy homeschooled the girls from day one. Both girls were very athletic, and Madison was even a national gymnast at one time. She was awarded a gymnastic scholarship to Auburn University in Alabama. During her first year there, she developed a serious physical problem that could cause the loss of a limb, or worse, death. Mark and Cindy pulled her out of the program, but the university honored her scholarship for that first year. However, she had to find somewhere else to go for her next three years.

Chelsea was great in athletics, as well, and was even head cheerleader at Liberty University in Lynchburg, Virginia. When Madison was looking for another college, she chose Liberty as well. It didn't take long for the two of them to form their own friendships, yet still have each other to lean on.

Eventually, both of them found their husbands at Liberty University. On June 11, 2011, Madison was married to a fine man named, Ryan Robertson, in the Thomas Road Baptist Church Chapel. Ryan was on staff at Liberty, and they purchased a home there in Lynchburg. Madison also worked at the university. Ryan is now youth pastor at Life Community Church in Greensboro, North Carolina. Madison works part-time for Zoo-Keepers Family Ministries, International, based in Jamestown, North Carolina.

Chelsea also married a fine, young man named, Tyler Harrison. The two had been on the cheer team together. Tyler was her lifter. Tyler is a physical therapist, a paramedic, and a fireman. Chelsea works for Foster Fuels, Co., based in Lynchburg, Virginia, as a graphic artist.

I've talked about everyone in my family, save one. That's my daughter-in-law, Cindy. Mark and Cindy have been married for thirty-seven years, now, and have a beautiful family. They have two daughters, Madison and Chelsea, and their husbands, Ryan Robertson and Tyler Harrison, respectively.

Now, they have two granddaughters, Madison and Ryan's little Reagan Jean, and Chelsea and Tyler's little Hayden Parker.

Ryan & Madison Robertson with Reagan, Mark & Cindy Andrews, with Hayden, Tyler & Chelsea Harrison

To go back a little way, I first heard of Cindy when Mark was a junior in high school and it wasn't long before the junior/senior prom. Mark hadn't been dating anyone, so I wondered if he would even attend the prom. So, I casually asked if he was planning to go. His reply was, "Only if Cindy Trantham will go with me." That was the first time he had mentioned her to me.

Well, he asked her, and she said 'yes'. From that point on, Mark had eyes for no one else. That was in 1974-75 and they were married on July 19, 1980.

About four or five years ago, it became necessary for me to make some drastic changes. I needed to move away from my home of 44 years. I assume that she and Mark discussed the probability of my living with them. Cindy very graciously agreed to share her home with me. This is no small thing. I know this because my mom lived with Floyd and I for 16 years.

Living with them has been wonderful! I have my own space, but complete freedom in the rest of the house to cook, wash clothes, etc.

I hear other women speak of their daughters-in-law, and often they are not very kind. But, I have only good things to say about mine and Cindy's relationship. I hope she is as happy with me as I am with her.

Cindy has many special qualities and talents. She is an extremely talented event planner and organizer that keeps her busy when she's not working in the lab as a micro-biologist. She is a beautiful woman who ages well, and I am proud to call her my daughter-in-law.

### *Our Musical Heritage*

On January 28, 1994, Mark and Cindy gave us a retirement party. We had sung gospel music for forty-four years. Hundreds of people came to Bryan Park Inn to help us celebrate, including our good friends Dr. Jerry Falwell and his lovely wife, Macel. I couldn't list all the people who were there if I tried, but it was a very special celebration. Our life-long friends, Dr. Ernie and Pat Robertson were there, our own pastor, Dr. Bill Kanoy, and his wife, J.E. Pigg and his wife Kathleen, and their daughter Charlotte. Also, most of the former member of the Gethsemane Quartet were there.

What a wonderful time we had! I will never forget it and will always be grateful to Mark and Cindy for all the trouble they went to in making it happen. It was a labor of love.

Altogether, in our forty-four years of service, Floyd and I made twenty-eight recordings with the different groups. Later, Floyd and I traveled together for ten years before the Lord called him home. We had wonderful years together and I will always treasure that.

We had many changes in our 44 years of service.

65

# Chapter Eight
*His Heavenly Flight*

On July 26, a typical, hot, summer day, I was scheduled to sing at Hunter Hills Baptist Church, for a city-wide senior citizens rally. Floyd had been sick for about three weeks, but he insisted that he go to the meeting with me. I urged him not to go; I knew he wasn't able. But, since it was our fifty-second wedding anniversary, he claimed he could make it just fine.

The church was well-filled with seniors from all over Greensboro. My sister-in-law, Maxine Brown, was among those who attended. I didn't want to leave Floyd behind to sit alone, but I had to sit up front, so I could be ready to sing when the time came. Maxine told me not to worry, that she would sit with him.

Dr. Junior Hill was the speaker that day. I remember Floyd and I speaking with him, at his book table, after the meeting. He has been one of our heroes in the faith for many years.

When we left there, on Monday, I took Floyd to see a kidney specialist. Dr. Davis. On Tuesday, I took him to see his heart doctor, Dr. Tilley. If he found anything wrong, he never let on. On Wednesday, we went to see Dr. Nadel. After doing another blood test, his diagnosis was that Floyd was getting better. This was wonderful news to hear, but he didn't get better. In fact, he got worse.

On Friday night, I found him in the bathroom, looking in the mirror, at something in his mouth. When I asked what he was looking at, he turned around and showed me something that looked like a blood blister inside his jaw. He said that he must had bitten his jaw sometime, but he didn't remember doing it. On closer observation, I could see there were blood blisters all over the inside of his mouth. I was very concerned and, when I wanted to call a doctor, he refused to let me. He actually became quite upset with me when I insisted that we call someone. I sat down beside him, and with tears in my eyes, told him how much I loved him, and that I was only trying to take care of him. He understood, then.

On Saturday, Mark and Cindy had planned a cookout, and had invited us, along with Ken and Jean, Cindy's parents. Of course, we just couldn't go; Floyd wasn't able. Mark told me later, that he'd had such a strong desire to come and spend time with his dad. He'd told Cindy that he was sorry to leave her with all the preparations, but he had to come see his father. He'd told the girls, Madison and Chelsea, to stay and help their mother, but they, too, wanted to see their Paw Paw. They spent two or more hours with us that day. I never cease to marvel at how God orchestrates the events of our lives. There is no doubt in my mind that He put into Mark's heart to come and see his dad that day, knowing that would be the last time they would be able to visit together in that way. I am so grateful, as is Mark and the girls.

The next day, Sunday, Floyd insisted that I go to church, but it was against my better judgment. I didn't want to leave him alone being as sick as he was.

We had some visitors that afternoon. Bro. Jack Lemons, our pastor, and his wife, Jean visited with him that day.

I did not leave him Sunday night. I refused to because I just couldn't bring myself to do it. He was so very sick. When he would have to go to the bathroom, down the hall, it was all he could do to make it there and back. We slept in the den that night, as we had done for some time, and I noticed that his breathing was strange. I remember that, for the first time, I was afraid he was going to die. I begged the Lord not to take him from me.

On Monday morning, he awoke, went to the bathroom, and returned to the den, holding his hand over the left side of his head. He said, "My head hurts so bad. I've never had a headache like this before."

"I'm going to call Grace Wagnor to come and help," I said. When I mentioned this, a strange, puzzled look came on his face.

"Honey, do I know her?" he asked

Just then, I knew something was going on inside his head. I didn't make an issue of it though, but I said, "Oh, sure you do. You'll remember her when you see her." And, he did. He also had trouble remembering his doctor's name, but he could still describe him pretty well.

Grace came and immediately took his blood pressure. She told me to call 911 and the emergency team was there very quickly. They worked with him for a few minutes, then Floyd got off the bed and walked to the gurney. I rode up front in the ambulance, taking him to Moses Cone Hospital. I had already called Mark, and he met us at there.

He and I stood on both sides of Floyd's bed in the emergency room, holding his hands and talking to him, telling him how much we loved him.

Floyd was able to talk to us for the first two to two and a half hours. After that, he could only nod that he understood what we were saying. At one point, Mark noticed that his dad was looking at the shirt he had on – it was a very bright orange with yellow print – and Floyd even seemed to smile. Mark asked his dad if he liked his shirt and he nodded that he did.

About three-thirty in the afternoon, Dr. Peter Ennever called Mark and I outside the emergency room. He informed us that Floyd was gravely ill and was not going to make it. Upon hearing this, I knew my knees would have hit the floor if Mark hadn't been holding me up. I've heard people say that their knees felt like rubber. Well, mine did. My legs wouldn't have held me up. This wonderful man, whom I had devoted more than fifty-two years to, was about to leave me. My heart and mind couldn't handle that. I felt like I was hovering over my own body, like it was happening to someone else, not to me. But, it was happening to me.

This is when Mark and I learned, for the first time, that Floyd's platelets were being destroyed by a viral infection somewhere in his body – we never found out exactly where – and his blood was flooding his brain and his body. The doctor told us that Floyd would go quickly, and he did.

At eleven forty-five that evening, Floyd's spirit took flight. He had seemed to want to hold on for several breaths, and as I sat there holding his hand, I noticed his reluctance to let go of his life. I stood over him, placing my face near his and told him that I loved him with all my heart, and that it was all right for him to go, and I would meet him in the morning. That was when he let go.

I have thought, so many times, that I would have loved to have had spiritual eyes, so I could have seen all that was taking place in that hospital room. I know there were heavenly beings all around us.

Just then, Robert Griffith began to sing very softly, "There waits for me a glad tomorrow, where gates of pearl swing open wide..." How sweet was the atmosphere in that room! All of a sudden, my whole life was changed. This man I lived with, and depended on, was no longer with me in the flesh. Thank God, I still had my family and friends to lean on.

His funeral was a celebration. Floyd and I had already planned his own service some time ago. So, everything went very smoothly and beautifully.

Several former members of the Gethsemane Quartet were there and formed a choir. I wasn't aware that they were going to do this, so it was a wonderful surprise to Mark and me. They sang, "Going Home" and "What a Meeting" so beautifully while Jean Pollard played the piano. Dr. Jack Lemons preached his funeral and Rev. Nila Souther and Alan Cox spoke about ten minutes each. Darius Stewart and Robert Griffith also said a few words.

Then, Mark, our son, read a letter that he had written to his father on Father's Day, June 20, 2004. This letter was given to Floyd about one month before he got sick. In it, he said everything a father would want to hear from his son. After he read the letter, Floyd instructed me to make several copies of it and see that one copy was put into the funeral arrangements and have Mark read it at his funeral. Little did either of us know that Mark would be reading that letter aloud within a month and a half. Here is a copy of that very letter:

Dear Dad,

Thank you for being a faithful father. I have always known that you love me, and have never doubted that you would do anything to protect, provide for and guide me. Always being confident of your devotion to me as my father has been one of the greatest blessings of my life. I think it's important for you to know that I have watched you intently and I remember. I remember the pony you got me because I had to have a real one. I remember how we kept him at Uncle Roy's. I remember the cart you had made so "Trigger" (named after Roy Rogers' horse) could pull us around. I can still see us riding in that cart just as clear as playing a video in my mind. I remember you picking me up from Kinder Garden. I can remember looking up from the playing ground and seeing my dad come to take me home. I can even see the car interior and you as you drove us home. I remember times when I went to work with you before school started. We would go to the TV Grill first. I would order hash brown potatoes for breakfast. I can remember the sounds and smells and the cook with that lazy eye. I never really knew if he was looking at me or not. I thought it was so cool to watch him crack and egg, throw the shell behind him and never miss the trash can. Then we would go to your work. I remember the powerful machines and the crane. I was never to stand under the crane. I remember walking between the yellow lines (so I would be safe) as we made our way back to the office. Everyone called you Andy, and they always made me feel welcome. I looked forward to visiting the office and seeing my Uncle Bascom.

I remember planting tomato vines between the shrubs in our front yard. I remember riding shotgun on the bus during our weekend trips. I remember the times we laughed. I remember singing and the great places we visited and the wonderful people we met. I remember the day I went to Bob Jones. You helped me carry everything to my dorm room. After getting things settled in you asked, "Do you need anything else?" I carefully surveyed the room and said, "No, I don't think so." That's when I saw your tears. I remember that.

I remember the fishing trips. I remember mealtimes around the table. I remember the corn, tomatoes and cucumbers fresh from our garden, and I remember talking about everything. I remember the joy you had in giving. I remember the Christmas cards containing very generous checks. Many people rejoiced over getting those cards. I remember you buying me my first car in 1976. I remember you giving me your car in 1993. Even the car I drive today, you bought for me in 1998. I remember how you helped many that came to sing with us in the quartet. Even to inviting some to live in our home. I remember the many times you asked me if I had old suits or clothes I wasn't wearing anymore, because you were always looking to help someone else. I remember Dean telling me, "I don't know how I would have made it during my back injury, if your dad had not been paying my rent." I remember being introduced to a struggling music major who said, "I know how you are. Your dad sent money to help me through school." There were many. I was watching.

I remember how you took care of Grandma Brown. I remember how she wanted to give you her house, but you gave it back to the family. I remember how you took care of Aunt Mil. When she was afraid to retire, you said, "as long as there is food on my table, you will have food on yours." You kept her house in repair, you kept her car running and you kept her freezer packed. And even when her health and mind withered, you were there to take care of her. I was watching.

I had to speak to an employee about responsibility a couple of months ago. As an illustration, I told him how you not only expected me to stay out of trouble with the neighbors, but you also expected me to be a peacemaker, even in matters where I was not to blame. I just had a mid year review with this employee and commended him for his marked improvement. He said, "I hope you don't mind, but I told that story about you and your father to my two sons." Then he proceeded to describe the experience he had in teaching his sons to be peacemakers. There is so much I have learned from you, and I'm still watching and learning.

I heard a pastor say how much he enjoys, at the end of a busy day, going to bed and getting rest. I could sure relate to that. Then he said, "God has a way of preparing us for eternal rest with Him." When we have done so much in life, there is joy in completing the race, but there also grows a longing for rest. I am thankful God has allowed me to still have you and Mom in this life. You are powerful sources of strength and comfort to me and my family. God will be taking you through paths I will one day follow. I am watching. I will be there for you, and you will again be showing me the way.

A faithful father touches more than just the lives of his children. He impacts his world. Thank you for being a faithful father.

Happy Father's Day!

I love you,

Mark


June 20, 2004

## Together Still

Let me hold your hand as we walk down the hill,
We've shared our strength and we share it still,
It hasn't been easy to make the climb,
But the way is eased by your hand in mine.

Like the lake, our life has had ripples too,
Ill health and worries, and payments due.
With happy pauses along the way,
A graduation, a raise in pay.
At the foot of the slope, we will stop and rest,
Look back if you wish, we've been truly blessed.
We've been spared the grief of being torn apart,
By death, or divorce, or a broken heart.
The view ahead is one of the best,
Just a little further, and then rest.
We move more slowly, but together still,
Let me hold your hand as we go down the hill.

- Selected

**Drawn by me.**

"And we shall walk through all our days with love remembered and love renewed."

## A Tribute to My Love,
## Floyd C. Andrews

On August 2, 2004, my life came to a sudden halt. The love of my life left me for a better place. We had shared fifty-two precious years.

Fifty-two years sounds like a long stretch of time, on the surface, but in reality, it was too brief. James 4:14 says, "For what is your life? It is even a vapor that appeareth for a little time, and then vanisheth away." We were together almost twenty-four-seven, and then suddenly, he was gone. My heart and mind had a hard time accepting his absence.

We shared a love that most people only dream about. He loved me with a love, as near like that of Christ to the church, as one could possibly get. He would tell me every day, sometimes many times a day, how much he loved me. He would say, "Mrs. Andrews, have I told you I loved you today?"

And, I'd reply, "If you did, it's okay to tell me again."

He would walk into a room, see me, stop and lift his eyebrows and, in that silly little grin of his, look at me like he was seeing me for the first time. Then, he would tell me how beautiful he thought I was and would ask me if I was married.

He wanted me with him always. If he was in the den, that's where he wanted me to be. If I was off in another part of the house, he would, soon, think of a way to get me back where he was. He'd call out and say, "Mrs. Andrews, what are you doing?"

I would reply, "I'm folding clothes," or "I'm watching T.V."

Then, he would say, "Why don't you get us an apple?" or "Why don't you get us a glass of water?"

To this I would laugh, and tell him, "Well, *us* doesn't want an apple, but I'll be glad to get you one."

This might happen two or three times, until, finally, I would stop what I was doing and go sit beside him in the den. Then, he was happy.

I must admit that sometimes, I would get a little annoyed with him, but never angry. This was only at times when I wanted to go out shopping or out to lunch with friends. He was very jealous of our time together, but he tolerated it because he knew I needed it. He just loved me so much that he didn't want to share me. Now, I appreciate how he felt in a way that I hadn't before. I know, now, that his every thought was to take care of me, and he did that very well.

We had great fun together as we traveled all over the country, and never got tired of just being together. We traveled all those years without ever having a serious accident. God was always merciful to us and Floyd was the most careful driver I've ever known. He never made foolish moves and he didn't speed.

He liked to tell people, as we traveled from place to place singing, that when he first saw me, I was a seventeen-year-old girl. And, he told the friend, who had invited him to church, "If that little girl wasn't married, I'd sure marry her." And, about two and a half years later, he did. Many times, after we were married, he'd look at me and ask, "Are you married?"

I'd reply, "Oh, yes! Very much so."

Then, he would tell me, "Well, I just thought if you weren't married, I'd sure marry you."

He was my friend, my critic, and my challenger. He challenged me to always do my very best, and he was my most loyal fan. If there was ever a woman who knew, beyond all doubt, that she was loved, it was me.

Floyd was a great man. He was the most generous, loving, and faithful man I have ever known. He sought out people who had a need, yet, he never waved a red flag or needed recognition. If there was ever a man who had the gift of helping, it was him.

I heard a preacher, on the radio one day, use the scripture in Ecclesiastes 11:1, "Cast thy bread upon the waters: for thou shalt find it after many days." I am, now, reaping all the benefits of the bread Floyd cast upon the waters of his life. It's now coming back to me. So many friends and recipients of his generosity and love, are now showering their love on me in appreciation for the things he did for them.

He bought many suits for preachers, missionaries, and friends. He would even give away his own clothes, that he could still wear, if he thought someone had a need of them. He also gave money to those who had a financial need. I remember when he bought Dave Compton, and his family, a car just to help them out. He would pay people's rent, buy them clothes, or buy furniture for their homes. He loved preachers and people in the ministry. He wanted to help them as much as he possibly could, and God blessed him richly for it. Now, he is enjoying his rewards in Heaven.

That same preacher, on the radio, said there are three types of givers. First, there is the flint giver. You have to stroke him repeatedly to get him to give. Secondly, there is a sponge giver. This giver has to be squeezed to get him to give. Lastly, there's the honeycomb giver. This is when giving just seems to ooze out of them constantly. That is the kind of giver Floyd Andrews was. It was his mission and the delight of his life to help others.

He was a wonderful husband, father, and grandfather. He loved his son, Mark and he expected much from him because he knew he had so much potential. There was nothing Floyd wouldn't do for his son, if it was within his power to do it.

He loved our daughter-in-law, Cindy, and his granddaughters, Madison and Chelsea. He was constantly looking for ways to help them or make them happy. He was so proud of all his family. As I've said before, Cindy is a micro-biologist, but Floyd thought she was his private nurse.

It was his joy to get Mark and Cindy their first house, and to mow Mark's lawn, or have it mowed. It wasn't because Mark couldn't afford to do it himself, but it was just another way to say, "I love you."

I wish he could have gotten well. I wasn't ready to give him up. I will miss him until the Lord calls me home. Like King David said about his son who died, "I cannot bring him back, but I can go to him." Maybe we'll all go soon.

It's a hard thing to explain when people ask how I'm doing now that he's gone. As I was on the phone with a friend, one day, the thought came to me for the first time, and I think it covers how I feel... "I've heard it said that when a person has to have an arm or leg amputated, even though they can no longer see the amputated limb, they still feel it as though it were there."

That is exactly how I feel about Floyd. I can no longer see him, physically, but I feel him with me always. And, he's in my memories every hour of every day.

## Up There Somewhere

Beneath the clear, evening sky
Gazing on the sweet by and by
A way up there
Far beyond that distant star
Is a land of endless glory
Where the host of Heaven are.

Up there, somewhere
Is a city pure and holy
Where my loved ones are
At home with Jesus
Far beyond worldly care
In that paradise called Heaven

Up there somewhere.
Beside the grave of a loved one,
With pain my heart was overcome.
But, the blessed hope guarantees
This is not the end.
There's a land beyond these shadows,
Where we shall meet again.

*Thank God for this blessed promise. Until we meet again on Heaven's bright shore, my love.*
*-Penny*

# Chapter Nine
*Penny for Your Thoughts*

What was my life going to be like, now? I could hardly remember when Floyd was not bigger than life to me. I looked to him for decision-making, direction, and stability in my life. Now, he was gone. I knew I still had the Lord and I am so thankful He was with me all the way. But, Floyd was that tangible part if my life. He protected me from having to make hard decisions such as maintenance on our home, our cars, our properties, and our finances. I was always a part of everything, but he was the final decision-maker, and I was happy with that arrangement.

We had sung together since we started dating in December of 1949. God had so graciously granted us a ministry in song with the Gethsemane Quartet, and we had been blessed to travel extensively, especially up and down the east coast, and as far as Texas, Ohio, Arkansas, Indiana, Louisiana, Alabama, and many other states in between. Now, what was I to do?

I was reading my devotions, on day, about two months after Floyd went to Heaven. This is what I read:

A man visiting a shop one day, listened to the potter describe the procedure of making a useful vessel. As he talked about the 'firing' process, he stressed the importance of leaving the vessel in the fire for just the right amount of time. A vessel that is removed too quickly, or left too long, was certain to be of no use.

The visitor noticed that there was no timer and became curious as to how the potter knew when to take the vessel out of the fire at just the right time. The potter then informed him that there is only one way to know when to remove the vessel from the kiln and that was when the vessel started to 'sing'. Apparently, when the vessel reaches just the right temperature it begins to make a sizzling sound that the potter called 'singing'.

When Christ was facing the fires of death and the betrayal of his friends, the Bible says that he and the disciples "sang an hymn." You may be encountering one of the greatest trials of your life today, and wonder how long you will have to stay in the fire. The Lord is our master potter and, when we learn to sing in the fire, is when we will be removed. The singing Saint is the one that has been mended and ready to be used.

No matter what difficulty you are going through, remember you are going *through* it and not *staying* in it. When broken vessels sing, the mending is complete. Jesus is the broken man that can still mend a broken heart!

(This came from my devotion book "Joy for the Journey "compiled and edited by Dr. Calvin Evens and Dr. Calvin Ray Evens)

God knew just what I needed to hear or, in this case, read, to get me going again. Matthew 6:8 says, "Your father knoweth what things ye have need of, before ye ask him." Thank God, He does. I need not have been concerned because God has kept me busy, and I am so grateful to be able to continue giving back to Him, the gift of song that He gave to me.

A few years after Floyd went to Heaven, I received a message from a Dr. Jimmy Vaughn. He said he would like to meet with me and talk about my life and ministry. I was delighted to do that! Little did I know, this wasn't his true intention.

To my great surprise, he informed me that I was to receive an honorary doctorate degree in sacred music. Imagine me, a doctor! Wow! This ceremony took place at my church, McLeansville Baptist, with my family and friends around me. I was awarded a framed degree and all!

I am so proud that they thought I was worthy of such an honor. However, as much as I do appreciate it, I find myself reluctant to mention it. God knows!

# Chapter Ten
*My Changes*

I have concluded that one of the hardest things for a mother to do is to lose the responsibility of a family, the care of her husband and children.

From the moment a child is conceived in her womb, the two are attached by more than an umbilical cord. That child becomes a part of you. They depend on you for food and protection. You are their everything. They respond to your every mood, and you to theirs.

When they are born, you are responsible for their nourishment, whether it be from your own body, or another means. You feed them, dress them, bathe them, comfort them, care for them, cry with them, and teach them to talk to you. They occupy your every thought, from morning to night, twenty-four hours a day, seven days a week.

You watch them grow and learn. You suffer with them through the difficult teenage years when they are desperately trying to discover who they are and why they're here. Then, you watch, with pride, as you see them find their way, especially as you see them grow into a Godly man or woman. You watch them as they grow in grace and Godly wisdom, serving and seeking God's will for their lives.

It all comes down to loss of control. This isn't a bad kind of control, but the kind that keeps things in order and keeps a family happy and well cared-for.

When my son, Mark, went away to college, I knew it would never be the same. He was going to have to learn how to care for himself, and he would learn that he didn't need me as much as he once had. He began to find completeness in someone else, which is how it should be. Truly, I was happy for him, but sad for myself.

Thank God, I still had my husband, Floyd, the love of my life. I was still needed and much loved. I was still the woman of the home and still had a measure of control.

Then, came the grandchildren, two precious, little girls, Madison and Chelsea. Because of their work schedules, Mark and Cindy trusted me and Paw Paw Floyd to keep them two or three days or nights per week. What a joy! When they went home, I counted the minutes until their return.

When it was no longer necessary for me to keep them, I went through another painful adjustment. Several years passed, and on August 2, 2004, I said good-bye to my darling husband. For more than fifty-two years, he had been the center of my life. Now, I had no center. Suddenly, my whole world fell apart. What would I do? I had never traveled this road before and I was totally without control. This was another adjustment.

Almost ten years, I lived alone. There were good times and bad times. Oh, yes, I could come and go as I pleased, but at what cost? I even had a measure of control during that time.

Then, one day, I received a notice that the D.O.T. was going to take my house, and portions of my land, to enlarge Highway 29 N. and Hicone Road. At first, I couldn't believe what I was reading. About two years later, it became a reality and major changes were in my future.

My home of 44 years

Acting on the information we had, Mark and I began to discuss our best options. Finally, it was decided that we would build onto their home, I would move to Jamestown, and live with him and Cindy.

Once again, I was faced with change and more loss of control. One by one, I saw the things I treasured slip away. Thank God, most of my furniture was absorbed by members of my family, making it less traumatic. At least, now, I can go to their homes and see my stuff again, thankful for the joy that the things brought me over the years. And, I'm happy that they can now bring joy to others.

I am, now, eighty-plus years young. Ha! I am most richly blessed to have made it to this point and still be able to come and go, to continue my music ministry, and enjoy my family. God has met all my needs, and most of my desires. He tells me, in His word, Psalm 37:3, "Trust in the Lord and do good, so shall thou dwell in the land, and verily thou shalt be fed." Verse 4 says, "Delight thyself also in the Lord; and he shall give thee the desires of thine heart,"

Okay, so I'm not in control, but that's a good thing. I've turned the reigns of my life over to a higher power, who loves me and wants the best for me. Psalm 71:18 says, "Now also when I am old and gray-headed, O God, forsake me not: until I have shewed thy strength unto this generation, and thy power to everyone that is to come."

I want my legacy to my family to be a Godly one. Every now and then, when little Reagan is acting up, someone will say, "Oh, it's just a Jean thing!" She is Reagan's other grandmother, who is my good friend. It's my prayer, and my desire, when she is older, and shows love and dedication to her Heavenly Father, that she will say, "Oh, it's a Maw Maw thing!"

## *You Shall See Your Children's Children*

We waited for nine years for our first grandchild. I must admit, I was getting older and getting anxious. However, when that day came, January 12, 1989, our prayers were answered. I can still remember how it felt when I held little Madison for the first time. My heart was filled with love and joy.

Fifteen months later, we were, again, blessed with another little, red-haired girl, named Chelsea. I didn't realize, until that moment, how much love I was capable of. All it took was one look, and there was instant love.

When Madison was three years old, May of 1992, their family was in California for Cindy's sister, Marty's, wedding. Madison was going to be the little flower girl at the event, and everyone was busy getting ready for it. Mark and Cindy had rented a second story apartment, and while Mark was out getting them some food, Cindy was doing her hair. The girls, only two and three, were safely paying on the bed. However, unbeknownst to anyone, the window, by the bed, had a broken lock and when Madison leaned against it, she fell two stories and landed on the concrete. Cindy immediately ran to her and she called 911. Madison had a hair-lined fracture and her right arm was broken above the elbow, the bone protruding through the skin. All I can say, is God protected her. She suffered no ill effects from the fall and even grew up to be a national gymnast.

When Chelsea was still in her baby carrier, the family went to Libby Hill for dinner. Her carrier was on the table, and somehow, it fell off onto the hard, tile floor on top of her. Of course, she cried and had a bump on her head. However, for the longest time, Floyd could not stop being concerned that she would have some problems from it. Thankfully, she didn't.

One day, the girls were both sitting on Floyd's lap. He said, "I sure do love both of you girls!"

Chelsea answered him by saying, "We love both of you, too, Paw Paw!"

Madison couldn't stand to be late. Every time we were getting ready to leave the house, she would plead, "Mee Maw, are we going to be late?" And, I'd say, "No, Honey."

One day, we were going to the Arts Center for their art classes. I got the same question from her and gave her the same answer. When we'd arrived, and were walking toward the door, she asked me again if we were late. When I replied, 'no', Chelsea said, "Well, then are we early?"

For her third birthday, Chelsea told us she wanted a 'Baby Check-Up'. Her Paw Paw asked her what that was, and Madison said, "It's a sick baby."

There was never a dull moment with those two!

## ... *And Your Grandchildren's Children*

There is no greater joy than having a little one around to put excitement into your life. I now have two little great-granddaughters. Ryan and Madison have little Reagan-Jean Robertson, and Tyler and Chelsea have Hayden Parker Harrison. Oh, how I love them!
I get to see Reagan often and she is a delight. She is so very smart. At the age of two, she can quote Psalm 23 with drama, sing her ABC's and count. She is in perpetual motion, even with her Bicuspid Aortic Valve problem. I pray that it will never cause her any problems. She calls me 'Maw Maw', and I love it!

**Ryan & Madison with Reagan**

One Wednesday morning, I was at CBS, standing in the church vestibule, when I heard a little voice saying, "Maw Maw! Maw Maw!" I looked down and saw this little one running for all she was worth, with outstretched arms to meet me. Now, you tell me, is there anything, in this world, that can top that? Not in my heart.

Now, I don't get to see little Hayden very often, but when I do, I can hardly keep my hands off her. Like Reagan, she is so beautiful. Her smile, at almost eight months old, is electrifying. She's going to be a real charmer. I'm glad she has Tyler's family, like Reagan has Madison's family, and Lynchburg is only a two-hour journey.

**Tyler & Chelsea with Hayden**

Psalm 37:4 says, "Delight thyself also in the Lord; and he shall give thee the desires of thine heart." I know this promise is true, because I've found it true in my life.

Floyd has been gone thirteen years, now, and, some days, it feels like it was only yesterday. Other's it feels like it's been a hundred years. In the beginning, I was so lost, but God has filled my life with His joy, His love, and His peace. I can honestly say that he has made my life better than I could have imagined.

One of my deepest regrets, is having to leave Mark at three months old and go back to work. I missed so much of his baby life, which still causes me grief. However, God has a way of making things up to us and giving us the desires of our hearts. One of those ways was giving me the joy of keeping Madison and Chelsea when they were babies. Now, I have the joy of seeing, and getting to be a part of, my great granddaughter's lives. And, I have the great privilege of spending quality time with Mark and seeing what a great and Godly man he has become. What a great husband, father, and grandfather he is! He and Cindy have opened their hearts and their home to me, and they make sure that my life is good. I am blessed beyond measure.

## *Another Penny, Another Thought*

Children are like a bar of soap. Squeeze them too tightly and they will pop out of your hands. Handle them gently. Just a thought.

**Mark & Cindy with Reagan & Hayden**

# Chapter Eleven
## *My Extended Family*

As I've mentioned before, I had two brothers. Bernon was born first on July 5, 1925, and Bascom was second, born on January 4, 1928. Three years later, I came along on November 27, 1931.

I can still remember the good times we had growing up. Of course, we had to make our own toys like wooden guns with clothes pins as a trigger and rubber strips as the ammunition; 'Tom-Walkers' out of string and tin cans; and, stilts with two tall boards with an added piece of wood to stand on. This made us a couple of feet taller!

My parents, brothers, sister, and me

We even made our own see-saws by placing a large plank of wood over an old tree stump. I can't stress enough just how dangerous this was, and it would probably be unlawful for children to try this today, but we had tons of fun with it. Ha!

We played chicken on the railroad trestle behind our house. This is, no doubt, another game that would be outlawed today. But, I was always careful not to have both of my brothers angry with me at the same time. I always had an ally.

I was the baby of the family for nine years, then on December 16, 1940, a red-haired tornado came blowing in. All tornadoes have names and hers was Linda Lea. She was a wiry, little thing who, not only took over as baby of the family, but also took over my life and my toys, destroying everything as she went. Needless to say, she wasn't my favorite person in the world at this time. But, time, and life, has a way of changing things. Today, she is not only my sister, but she's also my friend. She, and her husband, Joe, have been there for me in so many ways. And, she's also my shopping buddy!

My sister, Linda & her husband, Joe

Bernon and Bascom's families have all been caring and loving toward me, and I love them all dearly. They are all God's gifts to me. Here is our family...

Joe and Linda Brown Hill
Alan and Michele Hill
Sandra and Mike Walker
David and Meg Hill

Bascom and Bernice Brown
Ronnie and Sharon Brown
Doug and Gayle Brown
Bruce Brown
Cindy Jolley

Bernon and Maxine Brown
Judy and Art Schoolfield
Jill and Dwight Wall

Floyd and Penny Andrews
Mark and Cindy Andrews

*Bernon, Bascom, and Bernice are all deceased*

My brother, Bascom, & his wife, Bernice

My brother, Bernon, & his wife, Maxine

## A Godly Heritage

I love being a grandmother, MeeMaw, and MoMaw! What a joy these children have been in my life! Now that I have little great-grands, my family is growing, but all this had to have a beginning.

I had Godly parents that I loved dearly, Newby Carl Brown, my father, and Murtie Mae Stutts Brown, my mother were Godly influences in my life. My father was born in 1893 and died when he was seventy-four years old. My mother, born in 1898, passed away at the ripe, old age of ninety-one.

My father, Newby Carl Brown

My mother, Murtie Mae Stutts Brown

My father was raised in Chatham County, North Carolina, in a place called Brush Creek, or Brown Town, the youngest of five children. His father worked in a saw mill and we aren't sure exactly from where he originated, though at one time, he was in Indiana, which may have been for a job. Daniel Carl Brown was an unschooled man who could neither read nor write. The story says that Daniel was saw-milling on the property of Elizabeth Jane Whitehead Bray and Jeremiah S. Bray, who had three daughters. He saw one of the daughters, Margaret, and fell in love with her. He asked her father's permission to build a shack on their property and, when it was granted, he eventually married

Margaret. She taught Daniel to read and write. He was a devout Christian man and became a Godly writer.

Daniel Brown & Margaret Bray Brown

My sister, Linda has something that he wrote from his heart in February 1900. In his writing, it is plain to see that he deeply loved the Lord. Here is a copy of the script he wrote so many years ago...

Coles Store, 5. C. Feb 1900

The happiest are those who are willing to take the lowliest place. Self-conceit makes the misery of multitudes who might be cheerful and contented all the day long if they could learn to think less of themselves and more of making others happy.

A man can afford to spend a long winter of years under the chilling snow of neglect and abuse if only he can come out bright and cheery and full of hope like the grass in the spring. He can afford to be trodden under foot, and have the plowers make long furrows upon his back if affliction and trouble shall only give him simplicity of character and lowliness of heart.

In our ignorance and pride, we are constantly forgetting that the lowly things are mighty. God has given the grass strength to curb the sea and chain the avalanche and set the bounds of the desert. It is by gentleness that God makes his children great.

The silent sunshine is mightier than the roaring storm. The divine conqueror who has overcome the world made himself the servant of every man's need.

Pride is indeed strong, and it makes men do and suffer a thousand things which they would never attempt without it. But compared with humility, pride is weak and all the virtues and enterprises to which it gives rise, end in disappointment and sorrow.

Pride draws its strength from principles that are false and from sources that must fall. Pride exhausts itself against imaginary foes, and it rejoices over victories that confer no honor and provide no peace.

The great discovery of Christian faith is to suffer and be strong, to submit and conquer, to be filled all the day. Dying and yet alive, to wear the cross and win the crown.

Our true greatness begins not when we think more of ourselves, but when we think more of God, more of duty, more of making others happy.

If we were called upon to get out into the streets and highways, to stand in the noisy or manufacturing or market place, to enter the salons of fashion and mansions of wealth and to teach men as I might find them in either place, the first lessons of human happiness in the finest words, I would say: "Love thyself last, praise thyself never. Try more to interest yourself in others more than others in you. Envy nobody; despise nobody; be willing to take the lowest place and strive to make it the highest by filling it well."

When disposed to repine at your lot, and to grow weary in well doing, think of the manger in Bethlehem and who was laid there… think of the cross of Calvary and who was nailed there on… think of the crown of Heaven and who wears it. To be happy, to be humble, to learn how little reason you have to be proud, look down upon the lowly flower and the perishing grass and see what beauty, what glory God confers upon things that you tread beneath your feet. Hear the voice which says, "learn of me, for I am lowly."

Daniel Brown

With deep regret, I never got to meet Daniel or Margaret, but I will one day. Praise God!

My father was a Godly product of Godly parents, and he taught me to love gospel music. He encouraged me to do what I've done most of my life, to use my voice as an instrument of praise to God.

Now, I may not be able to tell much about my father's family, but I do know quite a lot about my mother's. Her father was Alexander Haywood Stutts, or Woody. He was either Scottish or German. Her mother's name was Minnie Mae Hunsucker Stutts. Together, they had six children. Three boys were older than my mom and one brother and sister was younger.

Woody was an artist and a school teacher. He also drank a lot and died at the age of thirty-five from some sort of epidemic. There is no evidence that he was a saved man, which makes me sad because I have no firm hope that I'll ever meet him.

Alexander Haywood, Minnie Mae, Baby Murtie,
Herbert, Charlie, and Lester Stutts

Minnie Mae, my name sake, came down with Tuberculosis when she was very young. She was ten years younger than Woody, so she was only twenty-five when he died. Therefore, the last two children were not Woody's.

When Minnie Mae got too sick to care for her children, her daughter, Murtie Mae, my mother, had to leave school at age nine and take care of her mom and four brothers (her little sister did not live after birth). Murtie Mae did all the cooking, washing, ironing, and everything else that needed to be done to keep a house in order.

As if that wasn't impressive enough, she had been crippled by polio at the age of two. Her right leg withered from the hip down, she couldn't bend her knee to walk, so she would sling her leg upward from the hip.

She was an amazing little girl who became a more amazing woman. She could make all kinds of beautiful things with her hands, and she was the best cook in the world. She had a beautiful singing voice and I like to think that I have inherited some of her strengths.

I have no doubt that I will see my father and mother around God's throne someday! Thank God for a Godly heritage. Here is a letter that I received after Mother went home to Heaven, telling me how wonderful she was. As you can see, she was just as wonderful to everyone else as she was to me.

October 5, 1989

Dear "Penny",

I'm getting ready to file your mother's death certificate with the Register of Deeds, and I just decided to write and tell you what wonderful memories I have of your sweet mother and her dear family.

Your family was like family to me. I have mental pictures of such happy times—your mother sitting on our porch laughing and swapping stories with my mother and us children staying nearby to listen and enjoy. Your dad and I laying on our stomachs in the grass, with his directing my singing while he played the harmonica. Bascom and I dreaming together, playing cars under your house. Bones and I trying to have the last word in an argument. You, as a pretty child, holding your bottle and twisting your dress with the other hand in your mother's lap. The wonderful surprise of having a red-haired doll in your family when Linda came and the jokes your daddy told about her red hair.

I'm very thankful God allowed me to share as much with your family and I share in your grief.

Please forgive me for not coming to visitation but I had a virus that day and waited until Sunday after church to go by the funeral home.

Come see us when you can.

With much love to you, Bascom, Linda, and the rest of the family.


Catherine

# Chapter Twelve
*My Legacy*

Sometimes, I wonder how my children and grandchildren will remember me. It's a given that they will remember me, but how? They, of course, will remember that I was quiet and reserved and of small stature. They will remember that I loved to sing and that I sang all over the country, spreading the gospel and sharing the word through song all over the world, thanks to radio, television, and the magic of the internet. It's still hard to imagine that, with the help of media and YouTube, my voice can be heard all over the globe.

My family will remember that I liked my jewelry and pretty things. Even when I was a little girl and had very little of life's luxuries, I still had a strong sense of my appearance. My mother said I nearly drove her to the breaking point as she dressed me each day. My hair always had to be 'just so', and if I wore a blue dress, I had to have blue socks and a blue clasp in my hair. White would only do if my dress were white, and so on.

They will remember that I played the piano. Looking back, I often chastise myself for not applying more effort toward the piano. However, my dad did keep me busy singing. That's not an excuse, just fact, and I have no regrets about that. Singing has been my way of giving back to the Lord something that He gave me, with a thankful heart.

They will remember lots of silly, little things about me, but they may not know the hours upon hours that I spent, and still spend, calling out their names before God's throne of grace. They may not know the depths of my love for them, though I may try to show them daily. The older I get, the more I am aware of the brevity of life. I think of how God loves me and gave himself for me, making me compare His love for me to my love for my family. I realize that His love is perfect and mine isn't, but comparing the two loves, while factoring in the human part, helps me to understand His love for me.

Finally, if they can remember me as a mother, mother-in-law, grandmother, and great grandmother who loved God intensely, and loved them unconditionally and eternally, I will have been successful. To God be the glory!

I may have had my name in lights for a short time, but when all is said and done, my greatest achievement in life will have been my family.

## Finish Well

One of my very favorite chapters, in the Bible, is the seventy-first chapter in the book of Psalms. Verse one says, "In thee, O Lord, do I put my trust: let me never be put to confusion.

I have known so many good Christians who, in their latter years, like King Solomon, allowed themselves to be drawn away, enticed by the world system and lose their Christian testimony, along with the reward. 'Let me never be put to confusion.' Karen Peck sings a song that challenges us as Christians, and charges us to 'finish well'! That's my prayer. How sad it would be to serve God for so many years, and then, at the sunset time in one's life, to lose it and go into Heaven 'so as by fire'. Verse nine of the same chapter, is my prayer, "Cast me not off in the time of old age; forsake me not when my strength faileth." And verse five says, "For thou art my hope, O Lord God: thou art my trust from my youth.

I have had a wonderful life. Just saying that make me think of a classic Christmas movie, "It's a Wonderful Life." George's beginning was a happy one as he met and married the love of his life, Mary. He had a good home, family, friends, and a good job. What more could a person want? But, life happened, and he almost lost it all, including his life. Happily, he did recover in the end.

That's a sweet, encouraging story that reminds us that this life is very fragile. Our adversary, the devil, is ever around, and, like a roaring lion, is ready to pounce and destroy all that we hold dear. We must be diligent, always aware that our battle is not with flesh and blood, but against "principalities, against powers, against the rulers of the darkness of this world, against spiritual wickedness in high places (Ephesians 6:12). Therefore, we must make sure we take on the whole armor of God, that we may be able to withstand in the evil day, and having done all to STAND.

At the time of this writing, all my family profess to be saved, except, of course, the two little ones, but right now, they are safe. I am confident that one day, they, too will be saved. My confidence comes from the scriptures: 1 John 5:14-15 says, "And this is the confidence that we have in him, that, if we ask any thing according to his will, he heareth us: And if we know that he hear us, whatsoever we ask, we know that we have the petitions that we desired of him." 1Peter 3:8 tells me that it is His will that all come to repentance. What more assurance do I need?

To my family, thank you for always loving me, caring for me, and making me feel special. I have spent many hours calling out your names before the throne of God. Let Him be your strength, your strong tower to run to in times of trouble. Isaiah 41:10 says, "Fear thou not; for I am with thee: be not dismayed; for I am thy God: I will strengthen thee; yea, I will help thee; yea, I will uphold thee with the right hand of my righteousness."

You are my treasure here on Earth and I love you with an unconditional love. I want all of us to be together in Heaven.

*Where your treasure is, there will your heart be also –*
*Matthew 6:21*

**The End.**
*Well, not quite.*

Made in the USA
Columbia, SC
26 May 2018